The Fastest Things on Earth

By Eamonn Corrigan

Published by The Child's World®
800-599-READ • childsworld.com

Photography Credits
Elana Erasmus/Shutterstock.com, cover, title page, 13; Thomas Wyness, 5, 29 (top left); scott mirror, 6-7; Dilomski/Shutterstock.com, 8-9; Erinpackardphotography/Dreamstime.com, 10-11, 29 (top right); Gerald Robert Fischer/Shutterstock.com, 15; photoyh/Shutterstock.com, 17, 29 (bottom left); Charles M Ommanney/Shutterstock.com, 19; Shutterstock.com, 20-21; Ted Sanders/Wikimedia Commons, 23; NASA/Wikimedia Commons, 25, 29 (bottom right); Vasin Lee/Shutterstock.com, 26-27, 30-31; Jan Garbers/Shutterstock.com, 28

ISBN Information
9781503877962 (Reinforced Library Binding)
9781503878495 (Portable Document Format)
9781503879034 (Online Multi-user eBook)
9781503879577 (Electronic Publication)

LCCN
2025938218

Printed in the United States of America

ABOUT THE AUTHOR

Eamonn Corrigan has been teaching curious kids about science for over a decade, which means he's answered approximately 47,000 questions about why the sky is blue and whether penguins have knees. (The answers: light scattering and yes!) When he's not writing children's books or in the classroom, Eamonn loves getting his hands floury while baking bread, whipping up delicious meals in the kitchen, and completely dominating his friends and family at board games (okay, maybe he loses sometimes, too).

Table of Contents

AS YOU READ, LOOK FOR MORE **AFFIXES**
-able, -er, -ible, -ish, -ist, -ment, -ness, -or, -tion, -ture, -y, bi-, tri-, uni-

CHAPTER 1

The Wonderment of Speed

Have you ever watched a race and felt excited? Speed is all around us! This book explores the amazingness of Earth's fastest things.

What makes something speedy? There are an uncountable number of ways to be fast. Some creatures have evolved special adaptations for fastness. A hummingbird's wings flutter so quickly they're almost invisible. Human technological development has also led to a lot of different equipment for going fast. There is the slickness of a speedy convertible or windy sailboats to cross the seas.

As we journey through this book, we'll discover some of Earth's speediest creations. Some will be recognizable to you, while others are so strange they might seem like a unicorn. But all of them demonstrate the remarkable speed of our world.

DID YOU KNOW?
The word "speed" comes from an Old English word, "spēd," meaning successfulness or prosperity. Being fast was a sign of goodness, even a thousand years ago!

A speedy pack of bicycle racers rush to their finish line.

CHAPTER 2

Swiftness in the Skies

PEREGRINE POWER

There are so many speedy animals in Earth's wilderness. Nature has so many incredible creations. But which one is the fastest? Look up! Earth's fastest creature might be flying above you in the cloudy skies. The peregrine falcon is the fastest animal on Earth.

When this **predator** spots food, it doesn't just fly like most birds. This unique hunter has a special adaptation. It folds its wings tightly to its body and dives rapidly. Diving downward, its feathery body can reach speeds around 200 miles per hour (388 kilometers per hour)!

Peregrines have bodies made for quickness. Their sleekness helps air flow around them. Special structures in their nostrils protect their breathing during the dive. The protection makes the dive possible.

Ornithologists call the falcon's hunting dive a stoop. During a stoop, a peregrine falcon is faster than many racecars! The falcon's vision is so sharp, it can spot a pigeon from far away. This makes these birds excellent at navigation. Once the falcon starts its movement, the prey has little chance of escape.

DID YOU KNOW?

All peregrines have a clear sh third eyelid they use when diving. These act as protectors, keeping the birds' eyes clear from a mixture of dirt and debris. Their extra eyelids also provide insulation from the windy air.

A peregrine falcon tucks its wings into a roundish shape during a dive. This incredible hunter can reach amazing speeds.

A STREAK OF SWIFTS

Some birds are not just fast—they're tireless! The common swift shows reliable endurance. Investigations have shown that these fliers can stay in the air for nearly ten months without landing! Even drowsiness won't stop them—because swifts can sleep for part of their flight.

Swifts have an extraordinary relationship with the weather. They spend most of their lives up in the air, even if it's windy, cloudy, or misty. Unfortunately, getting wettish on a rainy day can affect their expandable wings. Lucky for them, they can sense upcoming storminess and will fly around weather systems!

Swifts have curved wings that look boomerangish in the sky. They can reach measurable speeds up to 70 mph (120 km/h) when chasing insects. Swifts are very maneuverable, allowing for quick turns and sharp movements. These birds' ability to fly for long durations of time makes them some of the quickest birds at migration. The fastest swifts can fly over 500 miles (800 kilometers) in a single day! During a year, swifts can fly nearly 10,000 miles (more than 16,000 kilometers).

Swifts fly quickly and can travel very far in a short time.

HUMMING AROUND

Hummingbirds are miniature birds. But they show remarkable quickness! These colorful fliers can beat their wings up to 80 times per second. The rapid vibrations mean their wings look like invisible blurs to an observer.

Some hummingbird species, like the ruby-throated hummingbird, fly up to 30 mph (48 km/h). This may be slower than falcons, but their smallness makes this achievement incredible. What if humans could move at the same speediness relative to our size? We would travel faster than 500 mph (804 km/h)!

Hummingbirds' heartbeats are amazingly fast. Their hearts can beat more than 1,200 times per minute during flight. In comparison, a human's heartbeat is typically between 60–100 beats per minute. This rapidness helps power their tireless wings and incredible movements.

When hummingbirds sleep, they enter a state called torpor. Their heartbeat slows from a whopping 1,200 beats per minute to just 50! This sleepiness helps with their conservation of energy. It saves energy needed for their speedy daytime activities.

Hummingbirds are unique in their ability to hover perfectly still and even fly backward. No other bird is this maneuverable. They rapidly dart between flowers, helping with the pollination of flowers all over the world. **Botanists'** observations show the hummingbird's importance to nature. Many flowers would not survive without the stickiness of pollen and this adaptable little bird.

Too fast to see! A hummingbird's wings move with incredible quickness during flight. This creates a blurry movement that's nearly invisible to the human eye.

CHAPTER 3
The Fastest Runners on Earth

CHASING CHEETAHS

The cheetah is Earth's fastest runner. This silky, spotted cat can reach an unbelievable speed of 70 mph (112 km/h)! They are universally known as the fastest land animal. Their acceleration is amazing. The cheetah's furry body can go from zero to 60 mph (96 km/h) in only three seconds.

Cheetahs have special adaptations for their signature speediness and quickness. Their long, powerful legs enable their swiftness. A cheetah's flexibility and stretchiness allow its spine to bend like a spring. This makes its body expandable and compressible so it can take longer strides. Even its tail acts as a rudder for steering. This helps cheetahs change direction while running at high speeds. Their spotty appearance makes them recognizable to most wildlife observers and trackers.

DID YOU KNOW?

A cheetah's body temperature can rise to 105°F (41°C) during a chase! This overheating is the main reason they can only sprint for short durations. Their amazing speed is only possible because of their cooling system and temperature regulation. People work to protect these runners from dying out.

Cheetahs have long, spiky claws at the end of their paws. These work like a runner's spikes. They give the cheetah's paws better stickiness on the ground, making more surfaces grippable. This is a requirement so that cheetahs don't fall while running at high speeds.

However, their quickness comes with limitations and restrictions. Cheetahs can only maintain top speeds for about 30 seconds before overheating occurs. After a successful hunt, they must rest before eating. Cheetahs' tiredness and exhaustion make them vulnerable to other predators nearby. Their restrictiveness to run long distances shows the trade-off between speed and endurance.

This cheetah displays remarkable speed as it hunts dinner.

CHAPTER 4

The Speedy Seas

MANTIS SHRIMP'S POWERFUL PUNCH

The mantis shrimp might be smallish, but they're still one of the fastest animals on Earth! These colorful creatures live in warmish tropical waters. As predators, they have a unique ability that's truly unbeatable and unmatchable. To attack their prey, mantis shrimp strike with spring-loaded claws.

Their specialized front limbs can accelerate with the explosiveness of a bullet. The mantis shrimp's punch reaches speeds of 50 mph (80 km/h). This creates an unstoppable force and unbelievable impact. The movement is so fast that it creates **cavitation bubbles** in the water. This means they punched so hard, the water boiled! When these bubbles collapse, they get very hot and release a bright flash of light. This brightness is noticeable, even in murky water and cloudiness.

DID YOU KNOW?

Mantis shrimp have some of the most complex eyes in the animal kingdom. They can see types of light that humans can't, like UV light. The rotation of their eyes makes them speedy at spotting prey in the watery depths. Visibility and clearness underwater are no problem for them! An investigation shows they have 12 to 16 different color receptors in their eyes. Compared to humans' **trichromatic** vision with three receptors, mantis shrimp can see a whole world we cannot.

The mantis shrimp's adaptation goes even further. Different shrimp have specialized limbs for different tasks. Some shrimp are spearers. They have spiky spines on their arms. This lets them stab prey as they swim by. Some shrimp are smashers. They have bumpy and heavy clubs at the end of their limbs. These can be used to smash into the bony, hardish shells of their prey. Even the hardest shells are breakable for the mantis shrimp. The many adaptations of the mantis shrimp really amaze the marine biologists who study them.

This rainbow creature may look gentle, but it packs a powerful punch.

CHAPTER 5

Humans in a Hurry

RUN, RUN AS FAST AS YOU CAN

Humans may not be as fast as the cheetah, but Olympic sprinters show remarkable quickness! The fastest human runners can reach approximately 27 mph (almost 44 km/h). Jamaica's Usain Bolt holds the still unbeatable 100-meter world record of 9.58 seconds. This record was set in 2009. His powerful legs and incredible acceleration made him the speediest human in history.

Sprinters use special shoes with spiky bottoms for better grippiness on the track. The stickiness helps them push off with maximum force for the best acceleration. Their training focuses on explosiveness and alignment of their limbs for sleekness. Using a compressible pose, the runners employ their legs like big springs to launch off.

DID YOU KNOW?

Our fastest sprint speeds are achievable only for about ten seconds. After that, tiredness sets in quickly. Marathon runners must carefully manage their energy in a process called pacing. This ensures they avoid unrecoverable exhaustion before reaching the finish line.

Marathon runners display a different kind of speediness. While their top speed is slower, their pace is much more sustainable. Elite marathoners run at about 13 mph (20 km/h) for over two hours! Their tireless bodies are very durable. They train to use minimal energy with each step.

Marathon runners need flexible joints and lightweight bodies. Their respiratory systems have undergone adaptable changes. Marathoners' hearts can pump more blood with fewer beats. This helps improve their endurance and overall fitness.

Jamaica's Usain Bolt celebrates after his team wins the Men's 4 x 100m Relay Final.

THE LAND SPEED RECORD

The Thrust SSC (SuperSonic Car) is the fastest car ever made on Earth! This amazing machine holds the official land speed record of 763 mph (1,228 km/h), set in 1997. Its incredible achievement has remained unbeatable for over 25 years. This speedster isn't your typical car—it wouldn't be a record holder if it was. It is a jet-powered vehicle designed for unimaginable speeds.

The Thrust SSC's measurements stretch 54 feet (16 meters) in length. That's longer than a school bus! Its width is 12 feet (three meters). Its height reaches eight feet (two meters). This giant creation weighs about ten tons (20,000 lbs). The designer's vision required this sizeable construction to hold mega engines. It also provides toughness when driving at **supersonic speeds**.

Two Rolls-Royce Spey turbojet engines provide the propulsion for this beast. These engines are normally used in fighter jets. Their output was a measurable 110,000 horsepower. That's about 1,000 times more than a family car. The **bilateral** thrust allowed for unbelievable quickness.

DID YOU KNOW?

The wheels of the Thrust SSC had a rotation of up to 9,500 rotations per minute (rpm). Such force would have caused normal rubbery tires to explode! Engineers created special sticky, metal wheels with extra grippiness.

The Thrust SSC sits on the dusty desert surface after breaking the land speed record in 1997.

The driver of the Thrust SSC, Andy Green, needed exceptional bravery to handle this unstoppable unit. A test was done in the Black Rock Desert in Nevada. The flatness and emptiness of the desert environment made it ideal for fast speeds. Unfortunately, it also meant the race created giant dusty clouds from the dryness of the land. This made it hard for the driver to see where he was going. Despite these limitations, his skillfulness and preparation made the achievement possible.

The most amazing aspect of the Thrust SSC was its ability to break the sound barrier on land. It had been broken in the air in 1947. Another 50 years passed before this happened on land. Engineers and observers confirmed the supersonic speed by recording **sonic booms**. The fantastic speed meant the car covered one mile (1.6 kilometers) in just 4.8 seconds. Now *that's* fast!

This photo shows the dust that was created by the Thrust SSC as it broke the speed of sound.

Many organizations and corporations contributed to the success of the Thrust SSC. The project needed a lot of responsible testing and a flexible mindset. It took many versions to get the final design. Wind tunnel experimentation helped engineers predict airflow around the vehicle. All this hard work and dedication led to a truly groundbreaking achievement.

THE SKY'S THE LIMIT

Humans have dreamed of flight for centuries. The very first planes, which were made of wood, were very slow. In fact, the Wright brothers' first flier went only 6.8 mph (10.9 km/h). That's just fast walking speed! By World War I, pilots could fly 130 mph (209 km/h). Engineers and designers worked hard on making better engines and smoother curves.

A big change came with jet engines. These new movers made planes much faster than ones with propellers. The first usable jet fighter was finally built in 1944. It could fly at 540 mph (869 km/h)—a speed that was previously unimaginable.

BREAKING THE SOUND BARRIER

For a long time, many people thought planes couldn't go faster than the speed of sound. Some feared that the planes would just break apart. This created fearfulness among test pilots.

Chuck Yeager changed everything on October 14, 1947. He flew the *Bell X-1* rocket-powered plane faster than the speed of sound. His successful flight reached **Mach** 1.06, which is about 700 mph (1,126 km/h). The test plane was orangish and shaped like a bullet to help it fly at those amazing speeds.

Two days before Yeager's test flight, he fell off a horse and broke two ribs. Worried that he'd be removed from the test flight, he kept his broken ribs a secret. Unable to fully use his right arm because of the pain, he used a broom handle to help seal the plane door.

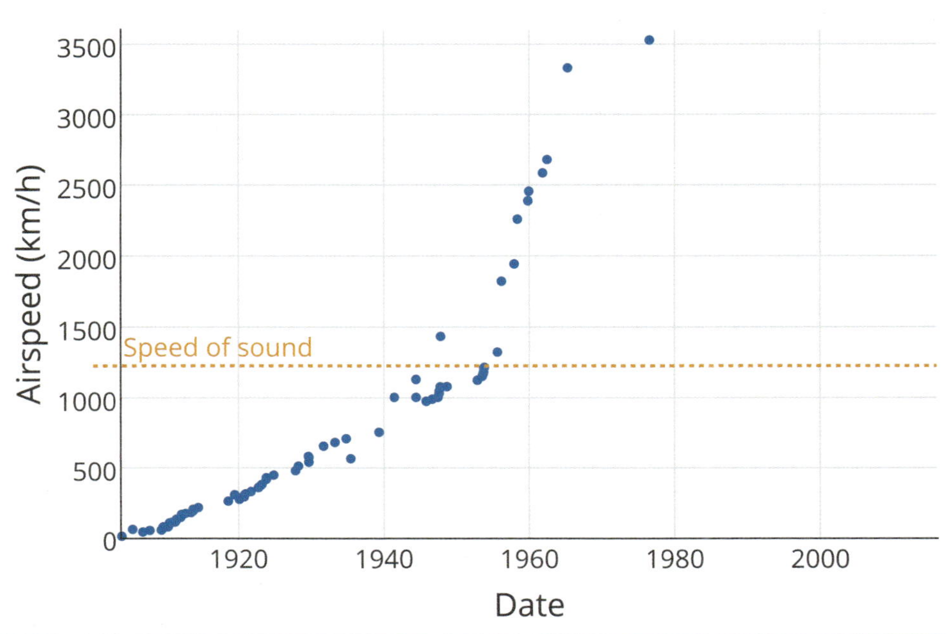

THE FASTEST PILOTED AIRCRAFT

The race for speed kept going during the Cold War. Today, the *Lockheed SR-71 "Blackbird"* still holds the official speed record for a piloted plane using jet engines. This remarkable jet reached Mach 3.3, which is about 2,193 mph (3,529 km/h) on July 28, 1976.

The *Blackbird* is made of titanium. That's so it doesn't melt from the heat of high-speed flight. Its engines work better as the plane flies faster—a truly wonderful achievement by engineers. Designed in the 1960s, the *SR-71*'s performance is still unbeatable by today's fighter jets.

BEYOND AIRCRAFT: HYPERSONIC AND SPACE VEHICLES

While planes that fly in the air are fast, space vehicles are even faster. The *North American X-15* rocket plane is the fastest piloted aircraft at Mach 6.7, about 4,520 mph (6,839 km/h). It's almost like a spaceship!

The fastest humans have ever traveled was in the *Apollo 10* spaceship. It zoomed at 24,791 mph (39,897 km/h) coming back from the Moon in 1969. The astronauts were moving about seven miles (11 kilometers) every second!

Newer spacecraft without people go even faster. The *Parker Solar Probe* orbits the Sun so physicists can study our star. As it circles closest to the Sun, it travels at 430,000 mph (692,000 km/h). At this incredible speed, you could go from New York to Tokyo in less than a minute!

Scientists and engineers are still working on faster vehicles. The development of these projects might change how we travel around the world in the future.

The launch of the *Apollo 10* spacecraft in 1969 is seen here. On its return from the Moon, the *Apollo 10* gave its crew the fastest ride a human has ever traveled.

CHAPTER 6

Nature's Triumphs

FAST AS LIGHTNING

Have you ever watched lightning during a storm? This electrical wonder is one of the fastest things you'll ever see in your life! Lightning travels from the rainy sky to the ground at about 270,000 mph (434,522 km/h). That's about one-third the speed of light!

A lightning strike has several parts. First comes the stepped leader. This is an invisible trail of electricity forming between the sky and the ground. Once the connection is made, this acts as a conductor. The return stroke races upwards from the ground. This creates the bright flash of lightning. The whole process happens in millionths of a second!

DID YOU KNOW?

Meteorologists' estimations say that lightning strikes Earth about 8.6 million times per day! That's about 100 lightning flashes every second.

Lightning is a very powerful radiator. It emits an enormous amount of heat and light—so much that no insulator could protect you. The air around a lightning bolt can reach 50,000°F (27,760°C). That's five times hotter than the surface of the Sun! The heat causes the air to expand like a bomb, creating the signature sound of thunder.

Speedy lightning bolts race across the sky during a thunderstorm.

SPEEDING AROUND OUR UNIVERSE

The observable universe contains countless unimaginable speedsters. One of the most remarkable fast movers are shooting stars. These chunks of rock fall from space, often traveling at nearly 160,000 mph (257,495 km/h)! This makes them some of the fastest measurable objects we can see.

A shooting star's incredible journey begins in the deepness of space. They can come from the dust left by comets or small rocks leftover from the formation of planets. They are whipped around our solar system by the Sun's gravity. They rain down on Earth with fierce speed.

When traveling through the Earth's atmosphere, shooting stars heat up and begin glowing. This is what produces bright, streaky trails that are observable to anyone looking up. The briskness creates such heat that most shooting stars vaporize before reaching the ground.

A time-lapse photo shows the bright streaks of shooting stars during a speedy meteor shower.

Bicycle racers

Hummingbird

AMAZING SPEEDSTERS

Look all around us, and you'll see speedsters everywhere. From marathon runners to lightning-fast supersonic jets, humans are always striving to go faster. But human power is almost no match for the speediness of animals. Nature can be very quick, whether it is the swiftness of peregrine falcons or the clip of mantis shrimp. Natural phenomena are also speedy, from flashes of lightning to the glow of shooting stars. Everywhere we look, we are surrounded by the speed of humans and nature!

Usain Bolt

Apollo 10

MORE AFFIX WORD LISTS

-able
achievable
adaptable
breakable
durable
expandable
grippable
maneuverable
measurable
noticeable
observable
recognizable
reliable
remarkable
sizeable
sustainable
unbeatable
unbelievable
uncountable
unimaginable
unmatchable
unrecoverable
unstoppable
usable
vulnerable

-er
designers
driver
engineers
faster
fewer
fighter
flier(s)
holder
hotter
hunter
leader
longer
marathoners
movers
newer
observers
racers
researchers
runners
slower
smasher
smoother
spearers
sprinters
trackers
travelers

-ible
compressible
convertible
flexible
incredible
invisible
possible
responsible
reversible

-ish
boomerangish
clearish
hardish
orangish
roundish
smallish
warmish
wettish
whitish

-ist
biologists
botanists
meteorologists
ornithologists
physicists
scientists

-ment
achievement
alignment
development
environment
equipment
experiments
measurements
movement(s)
requirement
wonderment

-ness
amazingness
brightness
briskness
clearness
cloudiness
deepness
denseness
drowsiness
dryness
emptiness
explosiveness
fastness
fearfulness
fitness
flatness
goodness
grippiness
quickness
rapidness
restrictiveness
skillfulness
sleekness
sleepiness
slickness
smallness
speediness
stickiness
storminess
stretchiness
successfulness
swiftness
tiredness
toughness
wilderness

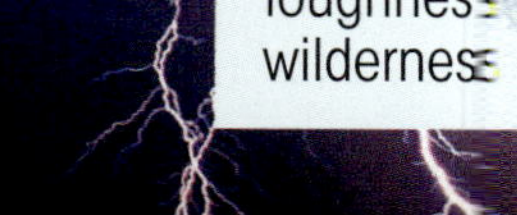

ctor
ˈor
or
tors
ɔr

ration
ation(s)
tion
ction(s)
rvation
uction
ations
ɔn(s)
ions
on
ɔns
ations
stion
mentation
mation
tion
gation(s)
ions
tion
ation

observations
organizations
pollination
preparation
protection
reactions
regulation
restrictions
rotation(s)
transformations
vibrations

-ture
creature(s)
future
miniature
mixture
nature
signature
structures
temperature

-y
blurry
bony
bumpy
cloudy
curly
dusty
extraordinary
feathery
furry
heavy
lucky
misty
murky
rainy
respiratory
rubbery
showery
silky
speedy
spiky
spotty
sticky
streaky
watery
windy

bi-
bicycle
bilateral

tri-
trichromatic

uni-
unicorn
unique
unit
universally
universe

GLOSSARY

bilateral (by-LAT-er-al): having two sides that match or are the same

botanists (BAH-tun-ists): scientists who study plants

cavitation bubbles (kav-ih-TAY-shun BUB-uls): small pockets of air created when something moves very fast through water

Mach (MAHK): how fast something is compared to the speed of sound; e.g., Mach 2 is two times the speed of sound

meteorologists (mee-tee-ur-AHL-uh-jists): scientists who study weather and make predictions about it

ornithologists (or-nuh-THOL-uh-jists): scientists who study birds

predator (PRED-uh-tur): a wild animal that hunts or preys on other animals for food

sonic booms (SON-ik BOOMZ): the loud noises created when something breaks the sound barrier

supersonic speeds (soo-pur-SON-ik SPEEDZ): any speeds that are faster than the speed of sound

trichromatic (try-kroh-MAT-ik): having three different colors

INDEX